Stay curious!

CURIOUS CRITTERS™
Volume Two

NATURALLY CURIOUS

With the success of the first volume of *Curious Critters*, I asked, "Why is a picture book full of animals talking directly to readers exciting the imagination—and piquing the *curiosity*—of so many children?"

In talking with readers, the answer became clear: Children love animals. Research shows that children have an innate tendency toward *biophilia*, the love of nature. Children as young as two are drawn to all things natural, especially animals. As much as ninety percent of children's dreams involve critters.

Children need nature. Take them outdoors. Read to them about nature. And focus often on animals. Help them explore. Encourage them to ask questions. Children are, after all, *naturally curious*.

For Olivia and Annabelle

All animals portrayed in this book were handled carefully and not sedated. Some resided at centers dedicated to education, conservation, and rehabilitation. Wild animals were returned safely to their habitats. A special thank you to the Alaska SeaLife Center, Ashland University, Back to the Wild Wildlife Rehabilitation Center, Brukner Nature Center, Gorman Nature Center, Jacksonville Zoo and Gardens, Ohio Bird Sanctuary, Toledo Zoo, and the Tom Ridge Environmental Center for opportunities to photograph animals in their care.

Additional Curious Critters: Harris hawk, front jacket flap; robber fly, page 1, lake sturgeon, pages 2–3; fishing spider, page 32; grapevine beetle, back jacket flap; gray treefrog and giant pacific octopus, jacket back; monarch, back cover.

Book design by Iain R. Morris.
Edited by Amy Novesky and Donna Linden.

Cataloging-in-Publication Data
FitzSimmons, David.
Curious critters: Volume two.
text & photography by David FitzSimmons.
p. cm. Includes index.

SUMMARY: A variety of animals common to North America pose for portraits against a white background while narrating distinctive aspects of their natural histories.

LCCN: 2013950090   ISBN: 978-1-936607-70-9

1. Animals—North America—Juvenile literature.
[1. Animals—North America.]
I. Title.   QL151.F583 2014   591.9'7

SIGMA
All photographs in this book were produced with SIGMA lenses.
To learn more about the photographic techniques and equipment used in making this book, please visit *www.curious-critters.com*.

CURIOUS CRITTERS™
Volume Two

Text and Photography by
David FitzSimmons

WILD IRIS
PUBLISHING
BELLVILLE, OHIO

MONARCH

Air traffic control, this is Monarch Flight 1 preparing for takeoff, flying from Milkweed, Minnesota, to Oyamel Fir Forest, Mexico. The estimated flight time for our two-thousand mile journey is just over two months.

We are looking at strong northwest winds carrying us today to an altitude of ten thousand feet. More migrating monarchs will be joining us along the way.

While we will not be scheduling return flights, our children, grandchildren, and great-grand children will be charting this same course—*but headed north*—next year, with our third generation flyers touching down in Minnesota mid-May.

Air traffic control, Monarch Flight 1 is now *airborne*!

INDIGO BUNTING

I love to sit atop fence posts, bushes, and trees . . . and sing!

Sweet! Sweet! Chew! Chew! Where? Where?

Other songbirds complain because I repeat myself, but I enjoy saying things twice, sometimes in very long songs.

Sweet! Sweet! Chew! Chew! Where? Where? Here! Here! Sweeter! Sweeter! Chew! Chew! What! What! Sweet! Sweet!

Other males in our song neighborhood sound the same, but, if you move to a nearby song neighborhood, you will hear different calls:

Chew! Chew! Sweeter! Sweeter! Chew! Chew! Here! Here! Sweet! Sweet! Sweeter! Sweeter! What! What! Sweeter! Sweeter! Chew! Chew!

In flight I call to my mate or other birds with a buzzing

Zeeep! Zeeep! Zeeep! Zeeep! Zeeep! Zeeep!

And when I'm bothered, I say

Spit!

PREDACEOUS DIVING BEETLE

Row, row, row my legs,
out across the pond,
look for fish, frogs, or worms,
I eat whatever's found.

Down, down, down I dive,
my prey I try to spy.
If my food is getting scarce,
I can also fly.

GREEN FROG

1 . . . Buuungk!   2 . . . Buuungk!   3 . . . Buuungk!

Hey! Who'sa here? I was justa gettin' finish'd up with my workout. Ya know, buildin' up my muscles for jumpin'
and eatin' and singin' . . . and *rasselin'*! Here, let me show ya my muscles *[flex, flex]*. Pretty strong, huh?

Sittin' here on the edge o' the pond, I'm always jumpy! Never know who's huntin' for ya.
And, trust me, if ya want strong jumps, ya gotta eat right. I chow down on 'bout anything:
insects, spida's, crayfish, snails, even otha' frogs. Sometimes I eat my own skin
after I shed it. *Hey!* If it's nutritious, I eat it.

Then, when I'm done eatin', I sing *[wink wink]* to the froggie girls:
Buuungk!   Buuungk!   Buuungk!

Hey! Ya boys out there: keep outta my territory,
ya hear? Swim all ya want outside my circle, but
if ya get too near, you'll hear me bark—*Grunk!*
Then ya'd betta look out: I'll jump
right out 'n' rassel ya!

Now, back to my exercises:
1 . . . Buuungk!
2 . . . Buuungk!
3 . . . Buuungk!

NINE-BANDED ARMADILLO

¡Buenos días, amigos!

Yo soy un armadillo. That means, "I am a 'little armored one.'" You see, I am small compared to my ancient relatives. Ten thousand years ago, my glyptodon grandparents were as big as cars. *¡Caramba!* I guess that makes me *muy pequeño. ¿Verdad?*

Now, my eyes may not be strong, but I can see you staring at my shell. *Está bien.* It's made up of bony plates called scutes, which help protect me from predators like hawks, bears, and coyotes.

People often poke fun at me when I am tearing up their lawns looking for food. They tell me to "scute" along. *¡Bah!* I just continue rooting around with my long nose, smelling beetles buried deep in the soil. Then I dig 'em up and eat 'em. *¡Mmm! ¡Mmm! ¡Delicioso!*

Well, I guess I will scoot along now. *¡Hasta luego!*

CAVE SALAMANDER

Do you want to go spelunking? You know, cave exploring? Well, grab your flashlight, and let's go!

Now that you've squeezed through the entrance, welcome to the twilight zone. Only a small amount of daylight shines into this part of the cave. See the stalactites on the ceiling and the stalagmites on the floor? I love to view them from up here, high on the limestone walls. I use my long tail, wedged into cracks, to help me climb.

Now we're in the dark zone. You may want to turn on your flashlight, but I just switch senses. I sniff for food— spiders, crickets, and flies—and feel vibrations when things move nearby. What's cool is that my prey can't see my long, sticky tongue coming out to catch them.

Speaking of cool, it's always about 55°F here in the cave, not a problem for a cold-blooded animal like me. But I'll bet you're ready to get warmed up. Let's wind our way back out, and thanks for spelunking!

BLUEGILL

Ahoy! Call me Cap'n Bluegill. I ply these waters looking for good eatin'. Me tall, flat body and me ruthless rigging—you know, me fearsome fins—allow me to sail smartly and steer sharply. If a snail, a worm, or a dragonfly larva dares to dally in me waters, I chase 'em down, then suck 'em in. *Gulp!*

Arr! The pond's like bilge water? Matey, I track me food in the murkiest muddle. That pinstripe down me side—it's me lateral line, a giant ear, fore to aft. It picks up vibrations in the water, like which way me dinner is swimming . . . or what scallywag wants *me* for dinner.

Shiver me timbers! Here comes a scurvy catfish. No—blimey—it's a squiffy turtle. I'll not be her dinner. Weigh anchor, me hearties, we're settin' sail!

AMERICAN ALLIGATOR

My brothers and I are practicing bellowing.

Rrrrrr! Rrrrrr! Rrrrrr!

We want to sound just like Dad. We're learning,
but our little lion-like grumblings are nothing
compared to his rip-roaring call:

RRRRR! RRRRR! RRRRR!

The quiet croaks of our hatchling
pod carry a short distance, but, let
me tell you, when bulls like Dad bellow,
Mom and the other females can hear them five
hundred feet away. That's what we want to sound like!

Of course, we're not always so rowdy.
Sometimes we simply breathe in loudly.

Hhhhh. Hhhhh. Hhhhh.

That sounds pretty eerie in the middle of the night when
we're up hunting. Of course, Dad's much better at this, too.
He sounds just like Darth Vader breathing.

HHHHH! HHHHH! HHHHH!

Well, it looks like Mom's ready to move. Voice training is over.
We are off to practice the "high walk." No dragging our bellies today!

SIDEWINDER

Hocus, pocus! Rodents focus!

Each and every day I perform my wild desert magic. Here's my routine: Wiggling into the sand, I vanish from view, disappearing from unsuspecting rats and mice. Only my eyes and the top of my sandy-colored body show.

When midday prey scampers my way—*presto-chango*—I transform dry sand into sidewinder *alakazam*. With a flash of fangs, the illusion is over.

Sim sala bim! The trick is blending in!

GOLD-GREEN SWEAT BEE

I love sweat! No, I don't mean I like to sweat. *I can't sweat. I'm a bee.* I like it when *you* sweat!

Did you just finish running? Are you nice and sweaty? Great! I'll clean you up. Of course, by "clean you up" I mean I'll crawl all over your skin and lick up your sweat. Flowers provide me with food—tasty pollen washed down with sweet nectar—and drinking sweat from your skin adds salt to my diet.

I should warn you, however: don't try to brush me off or accidentally squish me. Back there, on my *busy* end, I have a sweat bee stinger. It doesn't hurt a lot, but, I guarantee, you won't *bee* happy!

EASTERN BLUEBIRD

Knock, knock.

Who's there?

Blue.

Blue who?

Aw! Are you lonely? Don't cry. Two weeks have passed, and I'm ready to hatch. Here I come!

Pip . . . Pip . . . Pip . . . Crack!

EYED
ELATER

My name is eyed elater.
No beetle's jump is greater.

Click.   Click.   Click.

If on my back I've landed,
and upside down seem stranded,

Click.   Click.   Click.

I bend my back way under,
then click as loud as thunder.

Click.   Click.   Click.

Explosive upward swirling,
then toward the ground unfurling,
and somersaults uncurling,
only landing stops my twirling.

Click.   Click.   Click.

With luck, I end up standing,
my celebrity expanding.

Click.   Click.   Click.

I am the eyed elater,
glad to see you
later!

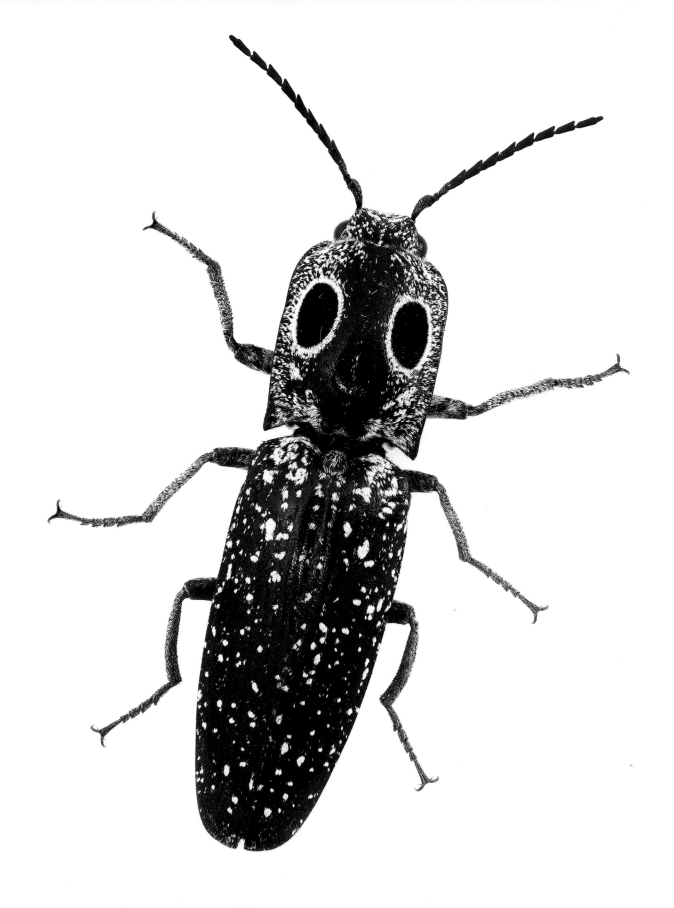

GRAY SQUIRREL

Listen, I *sound* like a gray squirrel: *Meeeehr . . . Meeeehr . . . Meeeehr . . .*

I have a bushy, blanket-like tail for keeping me warm in the winter, big ears for hearing predators, and swiveling hind feet for climbing down trees. So I *look* like a gray squirrel.

I even *act* like a gray squirrel, burying nuts in a thousand caches and then finding them several months later.

So, why do you think I'm not a gray squirrel? Oh, I get it. It's the *gray* thing.

I suppose that if I tell you that I am a gray squirrel, then you'll say I'm an albino. Yeah, yeah, everybody thinks that I'm an albino, but I'm not. Look at my eyes: They're not pink. I'm *leucistic*. That means I lack color pigments in my skin and hair, but, unlike albinos, not in my eyes.

So, I'm a gray squirrel . . . who happens to be white.

AMERICAN KESTREL

Ladies and gentlemen, boys and girls! For my next death-defying feat, I, Avid the Amazing American Kestrel, will fly to the harrowing height of one hundred feet, and, after attaining such an astonishing altitude, will hover magically in mid-air. Then, at the drop of a hat—*or the movement of a mouse or an insect*—I will dangerously dive directly downward!

And that's not all: after sustaining superlative speed, with earthly impact imminent, I will end my descent just in time, raising my terrific talons and taking my target. Drumroll, please . . .

Whoosh.   Whoosh.   Whoosh.   Whoosh.

Ladies and gentlemen, boys and girls! *Can you hear me from up here?*

Exactly one hundred feet high in the sky, I, Avid the Amazing American Kestrel, will begin my fabulous falcon feat, my death-defying dive. I have spotted movement. Here I come!

Sssssssssssssssssssssssswoooooooop!

CAROLINA GRASSHOPPER

What? You think I should be worried, sitting out in the open, in the dirt and stones? Nah . . . nobody's gonna eat me. My camo blends in very well.

Besides, my compound eyes are pretty sharp. I see all kinds of things, like good grasses to eat and where the lady 'hoppers are hanging out . . . or like you staring at me and that pesky old kestrel diving down to dine on me. No big deal. I just flip my hind legs, flap my wings, and . . .

Whzzzzzzzzzzzzzzzzzzzzzzzzzzzzzzzzzzzzzzzzzzzzzzzz!

NORTHERN CARDINAL

A couple of weeks ago my crested cutie and I flitted from bush to bush looking for the perfect spot for our nest. We found it, right in the middle of a tall, dense shrub. It took a week to build it. As I flew in with twigs, then leaves, then grapevine bark, and, finally, grass and pine needles, my singing sweetie put our cup-shaped nest together.

Then, after laying three eggs, my orange-beaked beauty began sitting on them while I brought her seeds to eat. A dozen days later, our hatchlings pecked their way out. They looked so cute!

But we weren't finished. We built another nest, and now the apple of my eye is incubating our second clutch of eggs. I'm feeding her seeds again, as well as stuffing countless caterpillars, katydids, beetles, spiders, and centipedes into the three gaping mouths of our ever-hungry hatchlings.

GEOMETER MOTH

Yes, it's true. I'm pretty good at math. Specifically, I'm good with measurements. For example, I can tell you that

5,280 feet = 1 mile

Normally, I don't measure things that are miles long. Rather, I spend my time measuring trees, usually while looking for leaves to eat. Trees are best measured in feet, but sometimes I measure branches or twigs, which are often less than a foot. I know that

12 inches = 1 foot

Speaking of feet, I have fewer feet than other caterpillars. Most have three additional pairs of legs—or prolegs— in the middle of their bodies. Not having these sets of prolegs allows me to loop ahead faster than other kinds of caterpillars. With each looping stride, I inch along. Therefore,

I = 1 inch

I am an inchworm.

EASTERN COTTONTAIL

So, let me get this straight: Mom's going out to eat . . .

Yeah, going out to eat and leaving us here for hours?

Yep. She said to stay in our nest, sit really still, and blend in with the twigs and grass.

Why?

Forget that. What about this running thing? Why can't we run in a straight line? Are we really supposed to zig-zag?

You mean never run straight our whole lives?

Well, Mom says it helps us get away from owls and hawks, foxes, coyotes, bobcats . . .

I'm scared!

Me, too.

Okay, I can live with being left behind while Mom eats out and with running all zig-zaggy weird, but, after we finish digesting our food and it goes through our bellies and all, are we really supposed to eat our own, you know . . .

Yuck! You mean we eat our own . . . *feces?!*

Feces? What are feces?

You know . . . *poop.*

Who said that?

I did. That's what I heard.

Yep. By eating grasses twice, we get more nutrients the second time through. All rabbits do it. What's wrong with that?

Eeew!

That's disgusting!

STRIPED SKUNK

Limerick
by S. Skunk

My skunk reputation's maligned.
On bees and small rodents I dine.
And that spray that you fear,
coming out of my rear,
I think odoriferously fine!

GREAT HORNED OWL

Shhhhhhhhh!

Look *Whoo Wh-WHOO Whoo Whoo* is coming to my dinner party, dressed in his skunky tuxedo and rhyming ridiculously.

I'd roll my eyes at you malodorous mammal, but, alas, my eyeballs are set in their sockets. So I'll just have to turn my whole head to look down at you.

Of course, I knew *Whoo Wh-WHOO Whoo Whoo* was walking through the woods. My large ears perceived you shuffling along.

At dinner time, some birds might wish they had better noses, but, the way I see it, *Whoo Wh-WHOO Whoo Whoo* is more fortunate than I am not to be able to smell very well?

Time to fly down from my perch now.

Ciao!

CURIOUS CRITTERS: NATURAL HISTORY

Monarch butterflies migrate up to three thousand miles. Adults west of the Rocky Mountains fly to the central California coast; those to the east head south to Mexico. Returning north, eastern populations lay eggs in Texas, with many of the new first, second, and third generation butterflies traveling farther north, often returning to the same locations inhabited by their predecessors.

Green frogs often sit along the edges of lakes waiting to catch food. With sharp eyes, excellent hearing, and strong muscles for jumping, green frogs often avoid predators, such as snakes, herons, and mink, by jumping into the water. Males, establishing circular territories ranging from three to twenty feet in diameter, attract females with calls that sound like the plucking of a loose banjo string.

Bluegill are abundant in lakes and rivers across North America. Their notched caudal, or tail, fin allows them to accelerate rapidly. Fanning the bottom with their caudal fin, males create saucer-shaped nests in sand or gravel, where females lay up to fifty thousand eggs. The male remains with the eggs, protecting them until the fry are able to swim away.

Indigo buntings learn to sing from nearby males, creating "song neighborhoods" of similar calls. While individual birds may live up to eight years, a particular song can survive for twenty years or more. Indigo buntings migrate at night, using stars to guide them. Internal clocks allow them to continually reorient themselves as the stars move across the sky.

Nine-banded armadillos may look slow, but they can move quite quickly. When startled, they may jump four feet in the air. Females give birth to identical quadruplets of the same sex. In the 1800s, Armadillos entered the United States from Mexico. Due to high reproductive rates and few natural predators, the armadillo's range continues to expand rapidly.

American alligators may grow to over thirteen feet and weigh more than seven hundred pounds. Besides hissing and bellowing, males produce a coughing-purring *chumpf* sound during mating season. When hatchlings are ready to emerge, they produce high-pitched noises. Alligator mothers then uncover the eggs, help their hatchlings out of their shells, and gently carry them by mouth to water.

Predaceous diving beetles have bristle-covered legs, allowing them to paddle through water. They breathe at the surface with two small openings, called spiracles, located at the tip of the abdomen. Underwater, the same spiracles draw oxygen from an air bubble trapped below their elytra, or wing covers. The larvae of predaceous diving beetles are known as "water tigers."

Cave salamanders use their long, prehensile tails to aid in climbing. They also use them to deter predators. Foul tasting secretions cover their tails, which they wiggle above their heads when bothered. If a predator bites the tail, the salamander is often not mortally wounded, and the bad taste turns away the predator.

Sidewinders move sideways in continuous "S" shapes, pushing themselves forward with only two small segments of their bodies touching the hot desert sand. Every time one of these rattlesnakes sheds its skin, a new rattle is added to its tail. A heat-sensing pit below each of the sidewinder's eyes senses prey in the dark.

Gold-green sweat bees vary in color, from green and blue to gold and copper. Living in groups like many other bees, they nest in stumps and logs. While only female bees can sting, males, if bothered, can pinch hard with their large mandibles. Sweat bees get most of their nutrients from pollen, but human perspiration adds necessary salt to their diet.

American kestrels are the smallest North American falcon. Living in various open habitats, including meadows, grasslands, and deserts, they hunt insects and small vertebrates, such as grasshoppers, sparrows, mice, and lizards. Even when one of these raptors is looking the other direction, two black spots on the back of its head make it appear to be staring directly at you.

Young **Eastern cottontails** remain in their nests for about two weeks, during which time the mother leaves to forage and returns to nurse them, usually twice a day. Eastern cottontails are coprophagous, meaning they consume their own feces—yes, their poop!—to get additional nutrition out of their food. They defecate two types of pellets, some for eating again and others for leaving behind.

Eastern bluebirds nest in tree holes and boxes. After laying a clutch of three to six eggs, two or three times each year, females lose a patch of feathers on their bellies. Like a warm pillow, this brood patch transfers heat from the mother to the eggs for incubation. After about two weeks of sitting, chicks begin pipping and emerge one to six hours later, typically at dawn.

Carolina grasshoppers, while supremely camouflaged at rest, startle predators upon taking flight both with the crackling noise produced by their wings and with their bright yellow wing bands. This bold coloration makes them look a lot like butterflies. Carolina grasshoppers stand on hot surfaces by changing which feet are down and which ones are up.

If bothered, **striped skunks** often stamp their feet as a warning before raising their tails and spraying two thin jets of foul-smelling fluid from their anal scent glands. If sprayed in the eyes, the yellow-colored secretion can cause temporary blindness. Because striped skunks dine on insects and rodents, this tidy, non-aggressive mammal is considered beneficial to humans.

Eyed elaters are members of the click beetle family *Elateridae*. That's why they are called "elaters." If stranded upside down, they snap a prong at the back of the thorax into a groove on the front of the abdomen, propelling themselves several inches upward. Besides somersaulting right side up about half the time, this click trick may also serve to startle predators.

Northern cardinals are among the most popular birds in North America. In most songbird species, only the males sing, but female cardinals call beautifully, often while sitting on their nests. This singing may be useful for females, allowing them to call to their partners, telling them to bring more food. Strong, conical beaks allow these granivores to crack open all kinds of seeds.

Gray squirrels are usually grayish in color, but some are born white. While a small number of white-colored gray squirrels are albinos with pink eyes, the majority are leucistic, lacking pigmentation everywhere but in their normal, gray-colored eyes. Although white squirrels may have trouble hiding from predators, people often protect them due to their unique beauty.

Geometer moths evolved to have fewer larval-stage prolegs—stubby, leg-like appendages behind their six true legs—than other caterpillars, which allows them to move faster than other moth larvae. Geometer moth caterpillars are commonly called inchworms, loopers, or spanworms. Their scientific name, derived from Greek, means "Earth measurer."

Great horned owls are powerful hunters. Besides preying upon rodents, frogs, and scorpions, they often catch birds and mammals larger than themselves, including skunks, for which they are the only regular predator. The stuttering, soft hoots of great horned owls advertise their territories. Breeding pairs often perform a duet of alternating calls.

CURIOUS CRITTERS
LIFE-SIZE SILHOUETTES

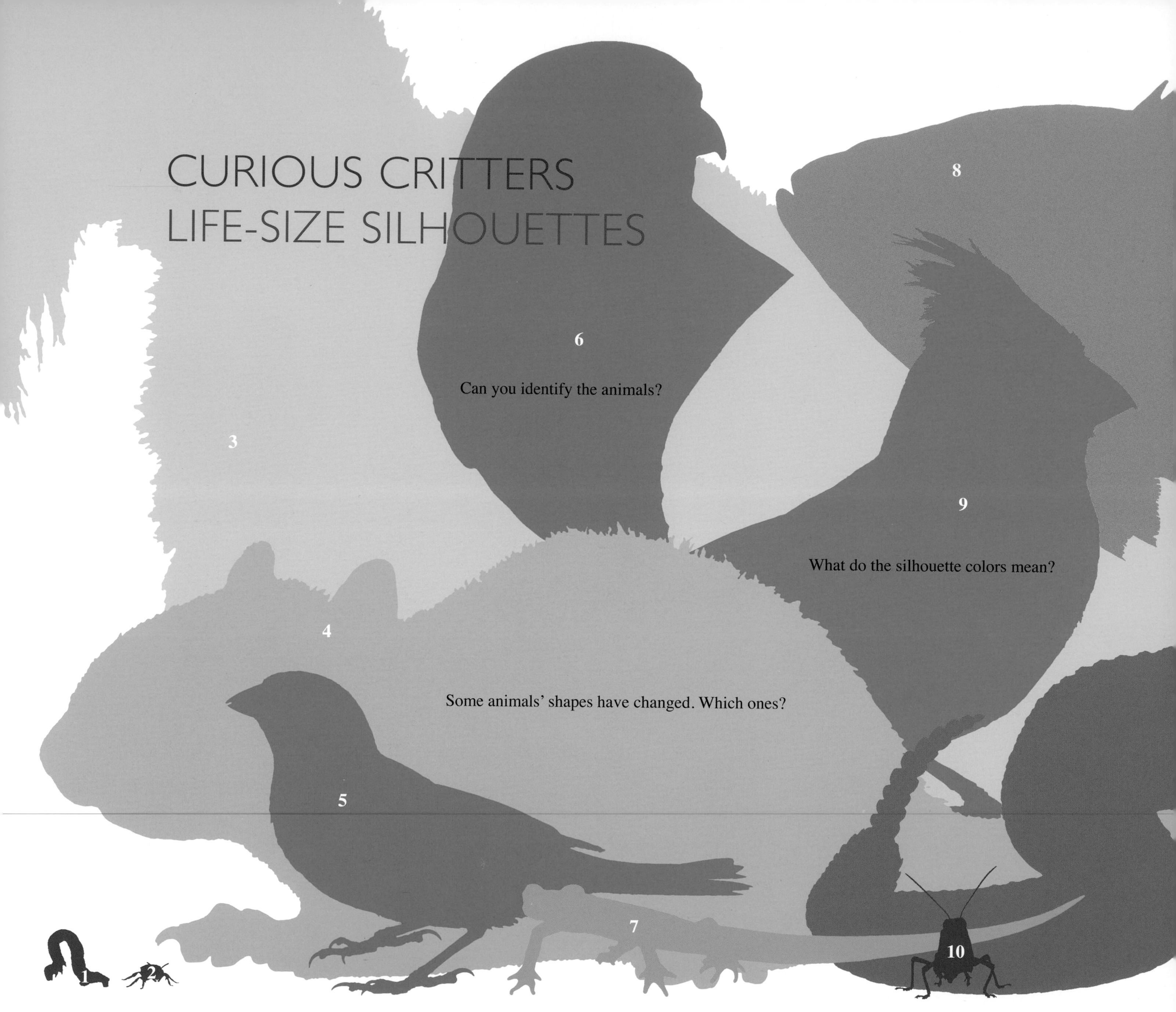

8

6

Can you identify the animals?

3

9

What do the silhouette colors mean?

4

Some animals' shapes have changed. Which ones?

5

7

1

10

13

Who is missing?

16

11

14

How many animals' silhouettes have been reversed? Which ones?

17

Answers are on the next page.

15

12

18

19

GLOSSARY

Abdomen: the rear-most body segment of insects, which contains most of the digestive tract.

Albino: an animal lacking the dark pigment melanin.

Brood: a group of young animals, especially birds or insects, born of one mother.

Brood Patch: a temporary, featherless spot on a bird's belly that conducts heat to eggs for incubation.

Camouflage: to hide by matching the appearance of one's surroundings.

Caterpillar: the larva of a butterfly or moth.

Clutch: a nest of eggs.

Cold-Blooded: of any animal except a bird or mammal, having a body temperature that varies with its surroundings.

Coprophagy: the eating of feces.

Dark Zone: the section of a cave into which no outside light shines.

Feces: waste material from an animal's digestive tract.

Forage: to search for food.

Fry: recently hatched or young fish.

Glyptodon: relatives of armadillos that lived during the Pleistocene epoch and became extinct about ten thousand years ago.

Granivore: an animal that feeds primarily on seeds.

Incubate: to maintain proper conditions for the development of organisms; in the case of eggs, primarily providing heat.

Larva: a juvenile stage of life of animals undergoing complete metamorphosis; plural: larvae.

Lateral Line: a system of sense organs in fish and other aquatic vertebrates, often noticed as a faint line running down the sides of an animal, that senses movement and vibration.

Leucistic (loo-SIS-tik): of animals, having reduced pigments in the skin, hair, or feathers but not in the eyes.

Metamorphosis: for animals, a change in bodily form through growth and restructuring.

Migrate: to move temporarily, often seasonally, from one region or climate to another region or climate that is more favorable for feeding or breeding.

Pigment: a substance in plants or animals that produces color.

Pip: of a young bird, to crack the shell of an egg when hatching.

Pod: a group of certain animals, such as young alligators.

Predator: an animal that hunts other animals.

Prehensile: of an animal's tail or limbs, capable of grasping.

Prey: an animal hunted by another animal.

Proleg: a stubby, leg-like structure found on certain insect larvae, including most caterpillars.

Rodent: group of smallish mammals with continuously growing front teeth that are used for gnawing.

Scute: a plate, sometimes bony, that is part of the skin and provides protection.

Spiracle: a small opening in the bodies of insects and other arthropods used for breathing.

Stalactite: a dripstone formation, resembling an icicle, found on the ceiling of a cave.

Stalagmite: a dripstone formation, resembling an upside down icicle, found on the floor of a cave.

Thorax: the middle body segment of insects, to which the wings and legs attach.

Twilight Zone: the section of a cave into which a small amount of outside light shines.

Answer Key to Silhouette Pages: 1. Geometer Moth (caterpillar), 2. Gold-Green Sweat Bee, 3. Striped Skunk, 4. Gray Squirrel, 5. Indigo Bunting, 6. American Kestrel, 7. Cave Salamander, 8. Bluegill, 9. Northern Cardinal, 10. Carolina Grasshopper, 11. Predaceous Diving Beetle, 12. Green Frog, 13. Monarch (butterfly), 14. Eastern Cottontail (juvenile), 15. Sidewinder, 16. American Alligator (juvenile), 17. Nine-banded Armadillo, 18. Eastern Bluebird (egg), 19. Eyed Elater

Four animals' shapes have changed: Cave Salamander, Eastern Cottontail, Sidewinder, and Striped Skunk.

Four animals' silhouettes have been reversed: Geometer Moth, Gray Squirrel, Indigo Bunting, and Northern Cardinal.

The Great Horned Owl is missing. To see the owl's silhouette, visit *www.curious-critters.com*

Silhouette Color Groupings:

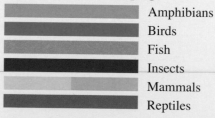

Amphibians
Birds
Fish
Insects
Mammals
Reptiles

Extra Challenge: Can you identify the Curious Critters not labeled in this book? You can find the answers on page two.

More Curious Critters are on the way! Games, educational resources, and additional photos at *www.curious-critters.com*